Healthy Me!

I GO TO THE DENTIST!

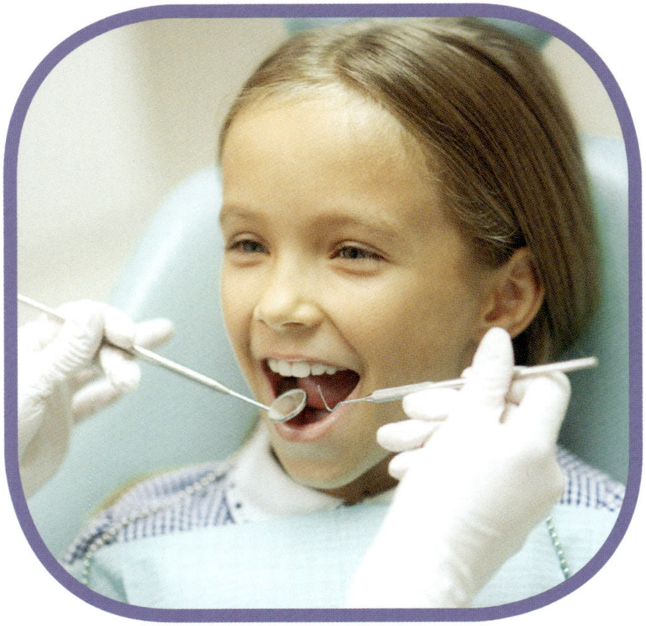

By Kathleen Connors

Gareth Stevens
PUBLISHING

Please visit our website, www.garethstevens.com. For a free color catalog of all our high-quality books, call toll free 1-800-542-2595 or fax 1-877-542-2596.

Library of Congress Cataloging-in-Publication Data
Names: Connors, Kathleen, author.
Title: I go to the dentist! / Kathleen Connors.
Description: New York : Gareth Stevens Publishing, [2023] | Series: Healthy me! | Includes index.
Identifiers: LCCN 2021037157 (print) | LCCN 2021037158 (ebook) | ISBN 9781538275443 (set) | ISBN 9781538275450 (library binding) | ISBN 9781538275436 (paperback) | ISBN 9781538275467 (ebook)
Subjects: LCSH: Dentistry–Juvenile literature. | Dentists–Juvenile literature. | Teeth–Care and hygiene–Juvenile literature.
Classification: LCC RK63 .C66 2023 (print) | LCC RK63 (ebook) | DDC 617.6/45–dc23
LC record available at https://lccn.loc.gov/2021037157
LC ebook record available at https://lccn.loc.gov/2021037158

First Edition

Published in 2023 by
Gareth Stevens Publishing
29 East 21st Street
New York, NY 10010

Editor: Kristen Nelson
Designer: Michael Flynn

Photo credits: Cover Olesia Bilkei/Shutterstock.com; p. 1 Dmytro Zinkevych/Shutterstock.com; pp. 5, 9, 11, 13, 15, 24 hedgehog94/Shutterstock.com; p. 7 Terelyuk/Shutterstock.com; pp. 17, 19, 21, 23, 24 wavebreakmedia/Shutterstock.com.

Printed in the United States of America

CPSIA compliance information: Batch #CSGS23: For further information contact Gareth Stevens, New York, New York at 1-800-542-2595.

Contents

I want to keep my teeth healthy.
I see the dentist.

Today is my checkup.
I sit in a special chair.

I have my teeth cleaned.

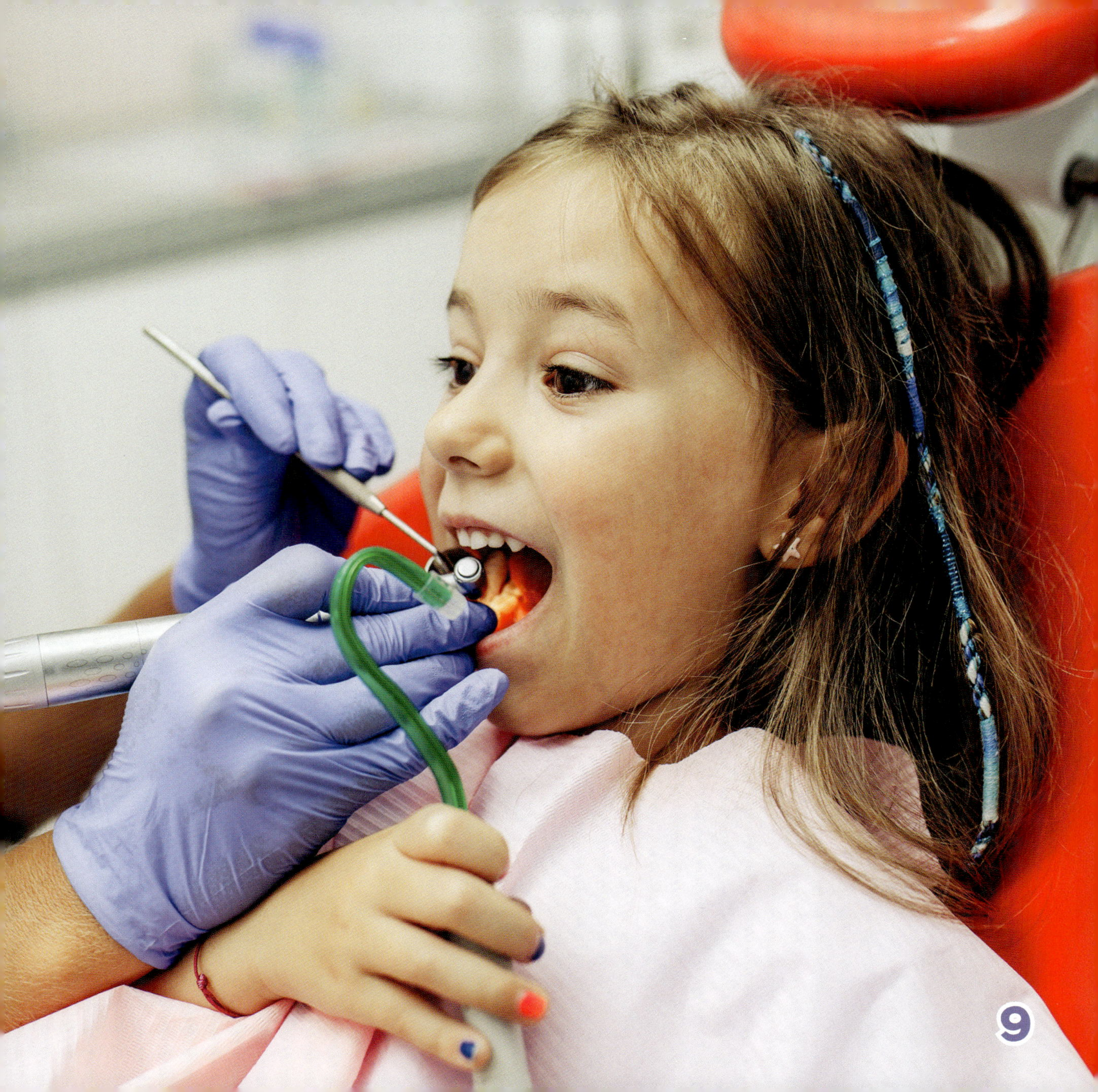

The dentist comes in.
This is Dr. Kendall.

She sees how my teeth
are growing.
She uses tools.

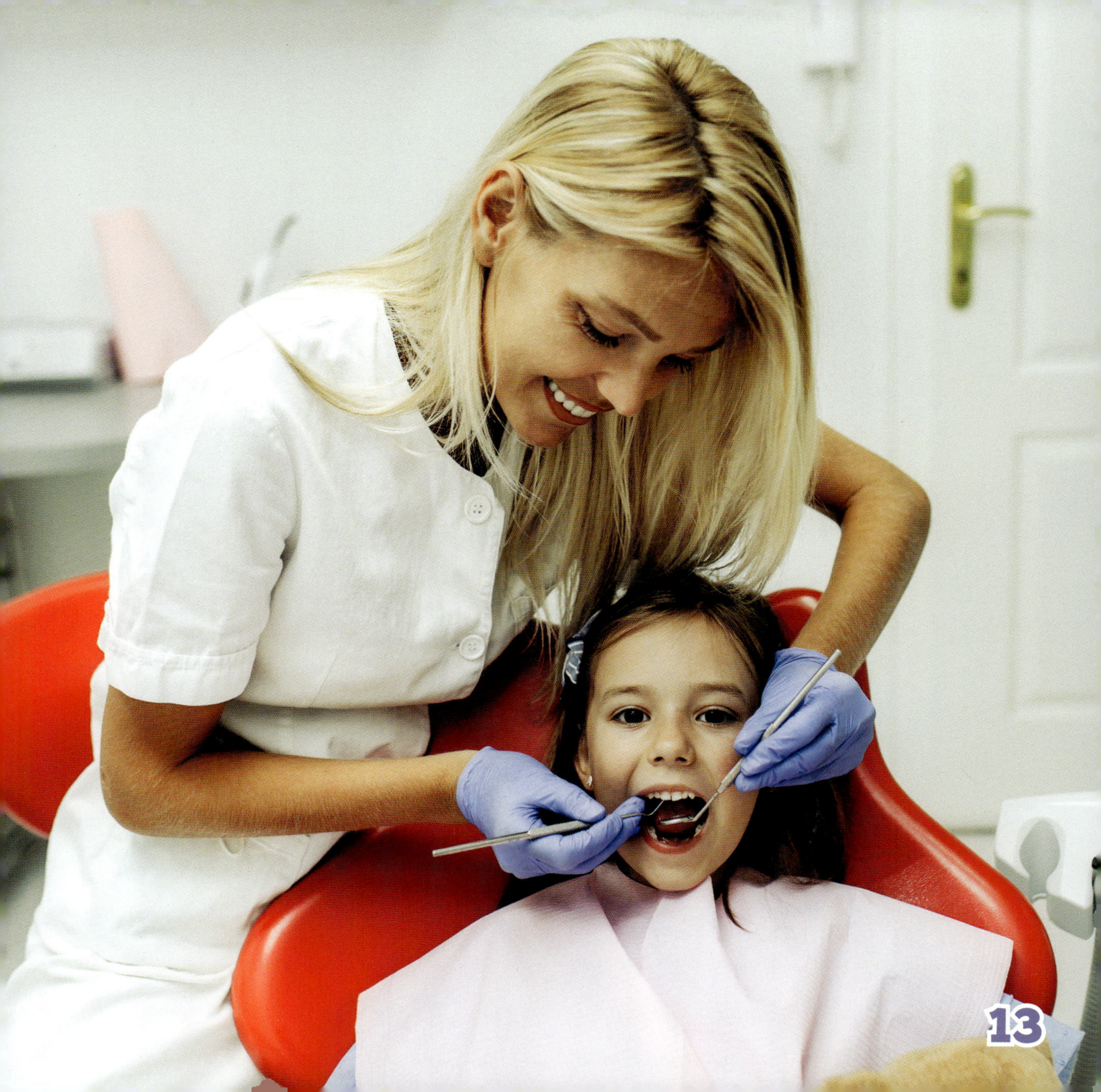

This is a mirror.
It shows behind teeth.

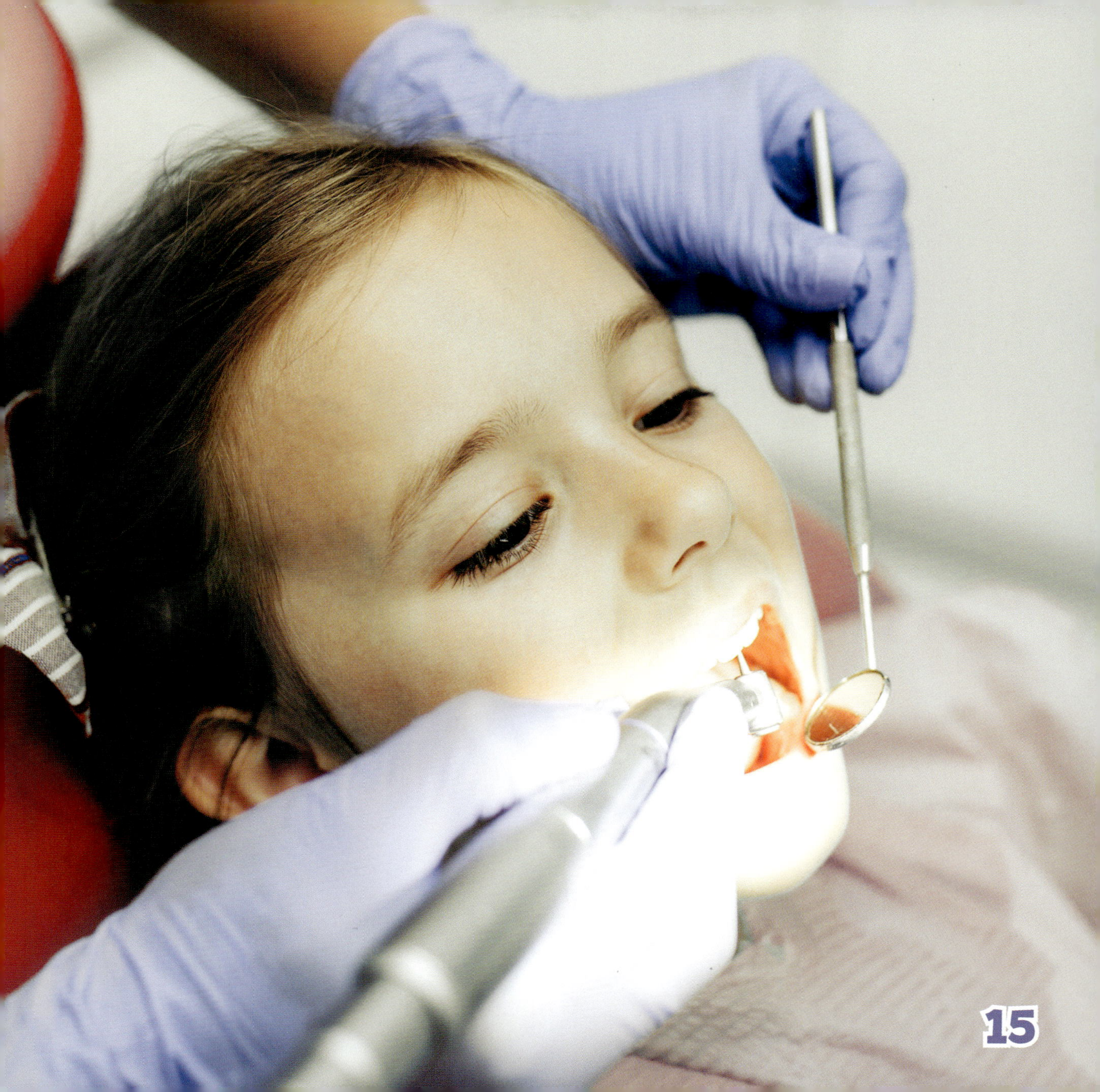

Frank's tooth hurts.
He goes to the dentist.

Dr. Suza finds a hole
in his tooth.
He fills it.

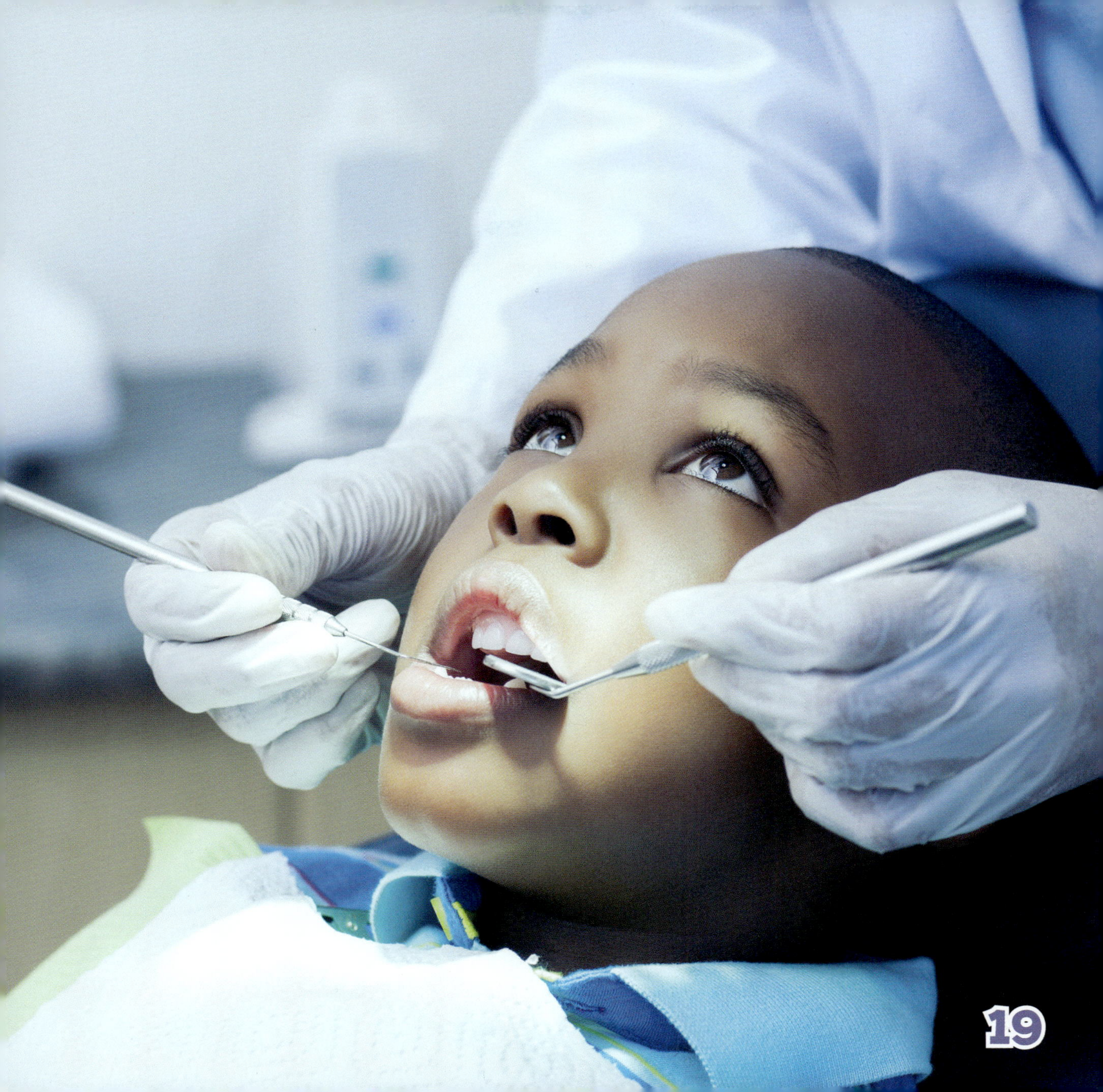

This is a toothbrush.
It gets food off
your teeth.

Now it is time to smile!

Words to Know

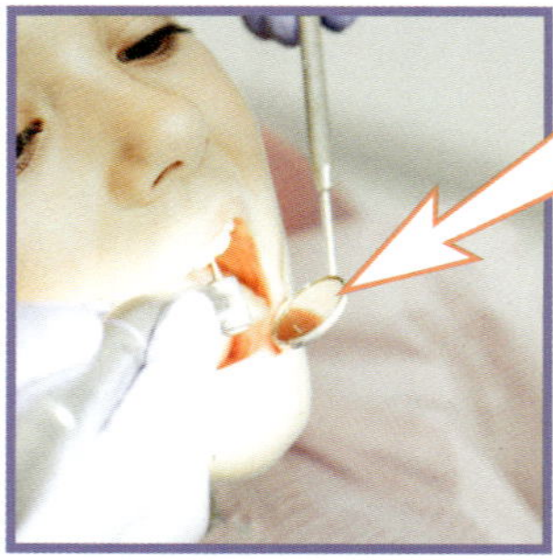

mirror

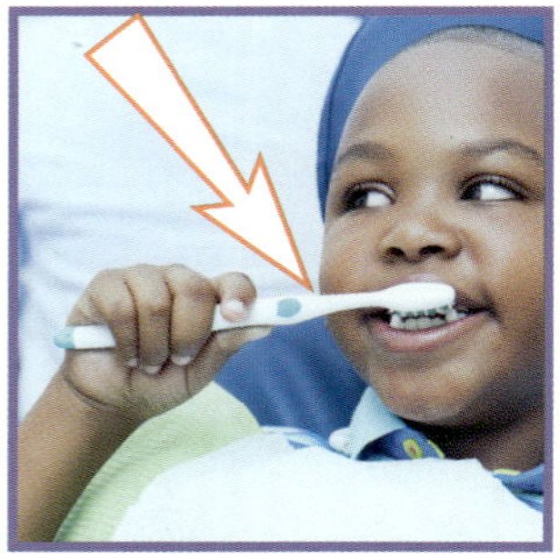

toothbrush

Index